Word Comix

ALSO BY CHARLIE SMITH

Women of America

Heroin and Other Poems

Cheap Ticket to Heaven

Before and After

Chimney Rock

The Palms

Crystal River (Storyville, Crystal River, Tinian)

Indistinguishable from the Darkness

The Lives of the Dead

Shine Hawk

Red Roads

Canaan

Word Comix

POEMS

Charlie Smith

W. W. NORTON & COMPANY

NEW YORK LONDON

For information about permission to reproduce
selections from this book, write to Permissions,
W. W. Norton & Company, Inc.,
500 Fifth Avenue, New York, NY 10110

For information about special discounts for bulk
purchases, please contact W. W. Norton Special Sales
at specialsales@wwnorton.com or 800-233-4830

Manufacturing by Courier Westford
Book design by Chris Welch
Production manager: Julia Druskin

Library of Congress Cataloging-in-Publication Data

Smith, Charlie, 1947–
Word comix : poems / Charlie Smith. — 1st ed.
p. cm.
ISBN 978-0-393-06762-0
I. Title.
PS3569.M5163W67 2009
811'.54—dc22

                                   2008037704

W. W. Norton & Company, Inc.
500 Fifth Avenue, New York, N.Y. 10110
www.wwnorton.com

W. W. Norton & Company Ltd.
Castle House, 75/76 Wells Street, London W1T 3QT

1 2 3 4 5 6 7 8 9 0

To Gerald Stern

CONTENTS

Word Comix

I Speak to Fewer People

I have been in touch lately with my inner self,
the fruit picker who lived all those years in a motel.
I shaded my story so it proved everything I did was
by intention. After each love affair, each participant
received a little gift. I mean someone always said:
You didn't really love her. I speak to fewer people
than ever. No matter what it looks like—I say this
every chance I get—something divine is going on.
And wonder: Is it? I'd like to lose a little weight.
Just the same, the marriage had its good points.
I still can't tell you what I am known for. I'm easily
shamed. On my walks I hope to meet someone interesting,
someone I have been headed toward all my life,
or simply someone without too much guile, a friendly
person with a little intelligence. Maybe we will
walk along together, talking about romance or trucks.

Evasive Action

. . . the clipped possessive moment, the barber on his porch
cutting his son's hair, who looks for a second straight into the sun
and then back at his son's head now a golden, nodulous remnant,
a flower if he likes or Lenin's bumpy skull, he puts his scissors down
and goes inside and apologizes to his wife, who doesn't understand,
but who accepts his words like a private harvest she's storing up,
and then the son, who's going into the army, comes in, half cut,
and sees them and thinks he understands years of bickering,
but doesn't, and goes on to the battlefield where he writes his sister
saying we are not far from the truth of things, watching beyond his hand
two scorpions pick at each other, and thinks of days by the river, of his
father recovering from cancer, singing a song his grandmother memorized in Vienna
and his father, who hated his own mother, cursing her, revoking the song,
and the next moment he's blown apart and then sent home in a metal coffin
and the parents and the sister get up early on the day of his funeral
and eat breakfast silently on the porch, and this is going on barber after barber.

Abuses in the Big Hotels

Small birds, damaged by shellfire, slant against the light.
"The descent of wisdom . . . ," the dictator begins,
and pauses, recalling his mother's wine-reddened face.
A residue of depression become ill will, a sensation
of engorgement, and an undeveloped moment in which the spirit stalls,
falls back and drops to its knees nervously trembling,
swing by. The old Cuban woman in the artist's photographs
seems less sinister today. Not long after midnight
sounds near the library like gunshots. The public yearns
for happiness, for exhilaration, instruction and seamless joy.
A frame-up fails. Light pours imprecisely over white coffins
tipped on their sides. An officer taking apart a man's face
regrets his lack of schooling. Acquaintances, called by the police,
resentfully clean the victim's apartment. A child is helplessly considerate,
misses what was said, wanders out of the backyard and disappears.
Grace naps in an empty garage. An illusion,
mistook for happiness, fades one afternoon about four.
The old man they watched six years straight do nothing yet
died between shifts. He left a bloody shirt once, in Tenerife,
and never went back for it. "I loved," the dictator says,
"the way my mother's body moved when she strolled along
holding herself in her arms. I have always loved
the elegant sway, the curve like infinity's cul de sac,
the seductive and unappeasable . . ." and stops talking.

One Lie After Another

I'd come so far, the last leg
in a shiny new car and then the ride on the special train

for the privileged & successful. A pigeon or a parrot
dressed up as a hawk with my fake beak

and tie-on sweptbacks and all. Then some brainiac
getting into the limo ahead of you, tossing

off a quip or saintly expression, something you never
expected: you stumble and glance up at the huge white buildings,

abruptly overcome. Why'd you even start?
You used to go around asking them how they did it.

How'd you get the motor going? What was it
you believed in? My buddy's a war correspondent now.

We lost touch after going sour in a poker game.
My ex-wife runs a store. Blah blah blah she used to say

when I tried to explain. Or *Help me help me.*

Smarty Pants

Even the most localized effects,
the sodden underwear

at the bottom of the
stairs, the corniness,

give way to a prehensive absolute
so shiny you'd think it'd outlast

the world. But
it doesn't. The capering prep cook,

a substitute, and his dumb helper,
a boy knocked

straight through time to this spot,
have more staying power (SP), live more fully

in the right now of dynamited redundancies and improvised
love affairs—

the little affairs I mean
in which some vagulous babe chucks a Chuck

under the balls
and goes whinnying into the night—

than any hopped-up proviso
discunted moralizers might devise, hon.

Evergreens

The year I admitted I was lonely
I didn't know what I was saying
       I said the nights are rough here
they have minikins & clowns
old postulates
taking out the trash and you
       get lonely sometimes. I didn't know
how one thing leads to another
like a smell under the house
       and then you're talking about the payoff
when you don't even want to
you want them to listen
like people with taps on their shoes
       who later as they heavily, roguishly dance,
think well of you.

The Paris of Stories

A specific passage in which the hero, painted blue,
howls in southern trees, that is, southern

France, and somebody says the City of Light
is this way, but you get close and it's getting darker along

the woody banks where statice and columbine
figure in a tale the apostle

of rationalism is telling to the converts,
who say this all happened before,

but then the apparent elaboration—the sunset, we mean—
striped like a figure of ridicule,

but brilliant, fucking sublime, the desperation turning to quality yellow
on our faces, the way

earth time includes these confusing generous passages,
gets to us, or to the one operating the ferry,

who leans back and lets his knotty fingers
trail in the water, thinking of his little life, so sweet to him.

Hollyhocks

. . . rosettes, or like those figs packed in a wheel:
hollyhock blooms stripped back to seed cases, summerworn capsules like tires
racked at a Gulf station in the dusty West of movies,
        the stems of these flowers known in roadside
Navaho gardens rubbed raw, frayed, strips of pale plant matter
hanging from them like Brian Donlevy's

collar shreds
(in *The Glass Key*)
as he dresses to do the worst
to get the best (time
        stuttering, smirking
its way out of the area, slithering), the stringy bits of coating

stripped from the peduncle,
        the tall skinny (stringbean) hollyhocks, and the
blooms *not like*
collar parts, or maybe studs (a spiky inflorescence),
rosaceous,
and Donlevy, like all of us,

secretly a hero, rugged
and noisy,
        filled with the lively force and animal good spirits

(Alan Ladd

his great fixer says, *He's on the dead up & up*)

     not always sufficient—I guess—

to keep us alive long enough

to bloom & proliferate, but must perish—we've agreed—

so it's not even a race, but only

a flowering, that fades—*one*

    after the other—leaving seed satchels,

wreaths, discs, coronals, festoons, chaplets & annulations,

not raiment, a springboard or destiny, but like those columnar starter lights

at drag races, flashing on in June,

      signaling summer's all clear,

the flowers tissuey yet slightly reptilian, *sostenuto*,

not spiraling, but set at intervals along the spike that's tough

and straight, the whole

shebang a fresh seeding

like a broken marriage you get up out of

and build a new life from, the attempt

to stay clear of what nearly killed you,

     like one gazing

at a dusty desert landscape

                  who sees hollyhocks

blooming in the old woman's garden

next door—signals they look like—the garden tipped,
spun around like someone hit by a car
thrown down busted in a ditch

        and left there, torn, little brilliant lights
and important points of elegance & forthrightness
done in, flowers

like the shed skins of small gods or Bikini Atoll
shambling back,

        those bushes
with their internal gizmos and genetic structures rattled
dazed and pummeled near to shit,

               maimed, little

Krazimotos, Igors, Ratzos

        and amiable mental midgets putting
forth a curtailed, counter radiance (like everybody), freakish,

like Alan
Ladd (imagination

& delicacy around the mouth, his
inability to miss
        what's really going on) revivifying
after William Bendix

beats his soul nearly out of his body,
the frayed
        and dying hollyhocks,
and the whole upended affair—
pattern scrambled—including the old lady's nondescript dog,
that, slowly,

like an aged *fabricateur* forgetting where he is,
                or not caring anymore,
Samuel Beckett (*por ejemplo*) in the nursing
home
glancing up from a last piece of work,
starting to forget

        the intolerable situation—turns his big head, the dog,
among the broken stems of great flowers—kings,

queens
mit regalia—

garden worn to the nap,

      the underdebris, (shredded, dry) like a bed now—

turns his head and—unable

to comprehend the works of humankind—looks at you (so you say—*we say we say*),

      tenderly.

Like Odysseus, Like Achilles

Homer sleeping on the ground,
little rock angle if he's lucky, goatskin
tarp, he's headed to some nobleman's

house for Thanksgiving, it's late in the season,
Homer's wondering
why at his age he's still thinking of women, doxies

he calls them, heartless charmers, he wants
to get up and pace,
but the boy's fast asleep, and truth is,

he knows it's not the girls,
it's him, his craving, these broads,
he can't shake the habit, the loneliness

and the harsh poetry of life are simply too much
w/out chicks in it, the disconsolation, you
name it: troglodytic personal ghettoism,

godforsaken secludinous isolato apartheid,
Maraboutian pillarist enmonkment & eremitistic adytum,
he could go on and on, but he never does,

he's just a country boy, simple and straightforward,
his heart like a used-up farmer
in a bad crop year, longing for a life at sea.

Little Swan Songs Being Sung All Down the Block

Consider the goodbyes you'd say to a baby in a satchel (*I got*
to get going now) the firebreaks broken through just in time
and the snarling child overrun by shame the unrestrictible
beauty of whole countries. Consider the rapidity
with which the world gets back to us the remarkably
festive nature of bridges in general. Consider how pigeon shadows
like black tears fall down the side of the Hotel W as you
grow more distant from possibility that is to say
are still on the killer's list. Consider please the
disputes settled by a glance the runaround still possible
mostly rescinded. Consider the refusal to let you in
the blasted heaths of love postmortems taking place in parking lots
and the rear projections of those—by themselves—falsely accused.
Consider the established way of speaking the unverifiable
particularities alluded to by a series of contestable affidavits
and a spiffy gent just cutting his eyes away. Consider
how dear the old man's look just was the subtlety uncapturable really
except if then in the royal flush of words if you were there to see it
the (consider this) still upright
moment beckoning like a tempestuous new lover just starting the tally.

Illustrated Guide to Familiar American Trees

I don't get it about the natural world.
Like, greenery,
without people in it, is supposed to do what?

City sunlight, I say, how can you beat it—
the walk to the pool after work, shine
caught in the shopkeeper's visor, bursts.

I see myself moving around New York,
snapping my fingers, eating fries.

My ex-wife's out in California.

I wish she was over on Bank Street,
up on the second floor,
and I was on the way there
to call to her from the sidewalk.

There's a cypress on that block, two honey
locusts and an oak. I love those trees
like my own brothers.

Winter Mornings in Kendall

. . . the streets become marginal
about now. Large gray tendencies just established
in the dark,
　　　　the aged bougainvillea pulling itself together
so you know there's going to be a world.

It's raining
on the other side of the bay. The addicts are
holding their meeting
on the beach.

　　　　(The day like a grim aftermath, refuse
and grime of night—battered, broke, *desangue*—Okay?)

It's damp,
cold in the courtyards of South Miami. Old ladies
stare blankly at their bruised thighs.
Guys in trucks eating yoghurt. You know some of them?

The ocean yesterday was smooth over lumps like a blanket.

It's the provenance of things
haunts some of us. What's next after the corkscrew?

Little fog curlicues
        swirl around the valves of the CO_2 tanks.
We got to get going, and soon.
The literalism of things—ah, I don't know.

The cats,
        this town's full of 'em, subtle stalkers,
bits of the old crepuscule, easing around the corner like the KKK.

Word Comix

People think I have a positive attitude,
but no, I'm one of the dusty breed,
like that exsenator hired to destroy China men
        who throws in a few women and sprats too

and keeps museum-quality scalps in a little malachite
inlaid trunk
        he opens at night for whatever whore he's consorting with—
and loudly grieves over—I'm like that,

        smalltime operator wearing his mother's underwear
        and divided against himself, as all operators are,
        a short man with backlit teeth,
        over-perfumed, in a personal sense,

        who asks himself in four languages if now he isn't ashamed,
ill at ease among friends,
cannonfodder, in a romantic sense, solemnicist, straggler
at the usual frontiers, unintentionally funny

in the past tense, spring-locked,
        Desdemonaesque (if she were playing Othello
in Shoney's Big Boy style), concessionaire w/out contract, ex-vocalist, fired
        on a morals charge—

An Orange Light in the Windows

. . . of course there are cranberry bogs for sale
and rich partial distractions
you experience when a neighbor's carried off,
poisoned by his wife. You say we all deserve it

or wash the windows and sit in the truck listening
to Crawdaddy sing his blues,
but the interference you sense, the dusty needle points
and delays in your release date

are real, as real as anything is. Where will it come from
this time? Your check's
lost like an expedition to discover
the source of the Nile. Speculation used to be fun,

but you're overextended, gripped
by nervousness now.
The rainout lasted for weeks.
And then an infestation of varmints,

something disassociated from itself, from the crew,
and things were hazy
and tasted of flavored salt.
Where did you put

the thingamajig that was going to save you?

A disputed set of values

didn't look right.

What did she mean, about the smell?

Materialism

. . . from where the pale blue and white extends
across the Hudson, accomplishing everything New Jersey requires at this time
by way of light and the subduing of light through the midhours, dusk,
the carious, infructacious shapes,
                    the solidities and structural
peculiarities of
commercial feasance and homes
for example of pharmaceutical executives sick to their stomachs
over money and love, or women
attempting to rage their way out of marriage, seem permanent,
but only seem, because nothing, blah blah, is,
not even the rocks at the bottom of the river
or the angularities
and approach of romance, or the facial expression by which you mean
I hate it, but I'll do it,
                or the way a man's mind drifts
when he thinks of the lake town in Florida
where he was arrested.
Next they'll be asking what it means to be alive.
On this side the half-pieced-together park stares straight ahead
from behind its barbed wire. The prison is outside the prison
is what they kept saying, but it was just to go on talking.

Child's Play

I got stranded down South America way,
drunk laid out
among Indian borrachos, drunk, couldn't care less.
We drank *postum*, or no, *posto*, a muddy
effluent squeezed from roots through bark cloth
into leaf cups and drank all day lying
back in the gloom of long houses out in the woods.
In those days no one came out to bother you,
it was OK to lie out drunk, conversing,
yelling a little, napping, staggering
away every once in a while to ogle the moonlight
or the grand scheme behind all things.
Some Indians, boys laid out by whatever lays drunks out,
and their buddies including me
for a few months I think it was,
down South America way, Venezuela I believe,
those years when instead of
playing Major League ball
I went another direction and had a devil of a time
getting to my feet.
It's remarkable how many poor souls
you run into there, jammed up individuals,
postscripts, locals w/out purpose and sometimes children
wandering the periphery,
looking for someone, you never know who.

Arthritis

. . . slow hitch and up pull of the hip,
the swing, knee barely flexing, the curve like

a sabal frond bent suddenly by wind, the foot flashing,
in a sense, forward, extended like the hood of a Bonneville, turned

slightly outward to catch with the face of the foot
the breeze, the Large Magellanic Cloud, to balance all there an instant,

the body upwardly following, appended, rising from the side
of itself like an architectural folly

or former city of light rising
from the excavated marl, the barely covered bones

aching all night, radiant like beacons
of a slow decay continuously occurring near us in the woods

out behind the mall, where boys with nothing else to do
run wild on Sundays, bellowing

and lashing each other with bicycle chains.

Out of the Way Bungalow-Style Areas

Sometimes love's vagrancy (whatever you call it)
overwhelms all but the most robust subscribers
and dishonest as it may sound the whole cramped enterprise
is given only a few minutes to clear out of town.

We were touchy that year, all year,
at least until the old lady died. Perhaps a singularity
enraptured you, caused the sell-off
and the false positive. Compare your notes

with the sample addresses, the ones
the boss started to give, but then just couldn't.
Outside the metropolis
you hardly find any restaurants worth eating in. Yet

the places are always full. Little families, conversation groups,
a sense of the fell and distracted nature of humankind,
the displaced circular reasoning one gets into after a gambling loss,
these show up, disperse among the tables

and fade into the background.
It appears we'll be here just long enough. For whatever
the thing is that knows no human reason to have its say. Or something
other, she explained, and passed the biscuits around.

As It Happened

Out in the snow
in bare places, windswept
behind filling stations in Vermont
on hillsides in the Maritime Provinces
by lakes where picnic benches
take up the thread of loneliness
the stillness behind
a remark recalled as one drives home
from the council meeting
the day
like an attempt to return
nonrefundable merchandise
dying in its own arms
the wind dying down
a softness in your wife's face
reminding you of something
you thought you'd never forget.

Monadnock

I'd say more about these rocks, but
there're limits to what we can know. You'd
think they oozed up
out of the dirt and how do you care for them
or come to know them in the way you know the community government.
From a distance they look calm. Scuff marks,
striations, frantically clawed areas, sulcations, ricochets
like tiny angels leapt up, depressions following this, muti-
lations, frankly crumbling spots, tiny
smoothed-off areas where makeup goes, notes
of lighter shading, nooks
where the mountain "spoke," half-
healed wounds where forces violently made them stop.
Bucket brigades, little
streams ladled from the top
trickle down. These rocks come up
from inside. The rains bring them out, huddled, close-cropped,
powerfully expressive, and so on, the splashed-with-white mass.
They form a trail. That's what we are talking about.
Ferns, firs, birches to either side. At the top, revelation
which is the point: there's a world beyond yourself.
Here you can see it. The valley, green or white
or red with burning brush
become expensive in your heart. You come up

with difficulty over rocks
and you can see things work like this,
the rocks appear "unchanging" and are obstacles
slow to wear away,
and then the trees loosen their grip, give up,
and you climb among blueberries and mountain grasses,
turn, and look freely out as if you are not imprisoned.
But you are standing on rock.

Summer in the Subtropics

I got interested in religion, licorice
and banana popsicles which signified the unusual
figurations of universal import, the carefully placed antecedents
and rabbity coverage we got in those days out in the sticks.
You get up and pray and
everything shelves away. The relatives smelling of swamp water
and licorice, the horses whinnying as if they mean it.
Then you try to believe what you're told. You get sores
in anterior cul de sacs. And after you finish the swimming lesson
they give you a popsicle. Does that explain it?
You think about her all day sometimes,
or like the time you said you didn't sleep
for fifty days, it seems like that. And now the arrangements
are going sour. They gather for their reunions—
we were never that close. And often from the background
made animal noises. Friendly animals, a little lost,
who might be coaxed out with a treat, at least at first.

Running in the Woods

The sprint downhill—these hints
of a fallen world—(frost
like proof of transformation) the thought

of a changed world
like an endless hope, but for what? Deer
stand among bluish shadows

waiting for the proper time to come forth.
One part of this preserve
prepares for another, leans

against pine & rock—
the early morning sounds, even this
far up the mountain,

like the almost quiet garden sheds of a
big city park, except
for the slight rustling over there

that isn't human. You're just standing
around in it, these woods.
The big trucks

parked over the hill grumble & throb.
The last green like a mop
shook out, dust all

over the grass—frost this morning.
You keep trying to hold your meanness back,
to change it, even

here where the woods,
so finite and easily shaken, mean nothing to you
and the people aren't friends.

Lariats

I suppose I want forgiveness for lying so bluntly
and not getting around behind the house
where the real work is, and I guess
I never got used to the suppositions
and colorful descriptions of harmonious doings
at the cotton gin or ancient château become a famous hotel.

The designs I had of random placement, of particular amenities,
passed with the night. I go where the fruit cups are.

Now the descriptions I read in the paper
of souls caught thieving, caught lying
about the body, always fit, always ring true.

I bought a car in Alabama
and drove it to Texas, traded it for a horse
and crossed into Mexico where I got arrested and sent back in a van
to Brownsville, put in a dormitory-style jail
and, after roughing up by agencies unleavened by courtesy, got out
on a hot dawn and sat in a café eating hominy soup,
thinking of Kafka, and Henry Miller who
in his great books never mentioned visiting churches or the Louvre,
and wondered how my horse was, an ignoble, bitter animal I disliked.

Oh Yeah

Afterward my friend explains
how awkward it is for him when there's no set procedure
and like a country maddened by grief
where the populace runs shrieking into the jungle
he is forced to make conversation
with some man he has no control of, like the time in New Orleans
when his wife rolled the Mercedes and showed up
with half her hair burned off cursing the police,
or he was just standing there, he said, like a god, *Christ*
you should've seen me, and this nut started talking about
his farm in Mexico, and suddenly my friend sensed
no one knew anything, really, about how to keep loving
anyone, anyone at all,
and that's how you get off on these little fishing trips
where you lie in the tent by yourself reading
the journals of lost explorers, and without looking
you can sense the sun, the spectacular evaporate,
erasing everything, that's how you take it, personally,
as if a secret shelter is slowly being exposed to scrutiny
or the joke's starting to make sense.

If I Wasn't So Mean

I'd get a turtle and raise it like
a fabulous potentate, like I'd wish
to be raised, a sacred ruler
without duties beyond what he thought up,
but I *am* so mean, and once kept as a pet a turtle
I found in the road, an escapee
obviously that I would have turned in
if pressured but instead
brought home and gave the run of the place,
but this turtle, this
reptile, who barely touched the lettuce
and tomato sandwiches
and preferred the dark behind the couch,
hissed whenever I came near
and smelled like he was defecating
small rotted corpses,
so—it was summer, brilliant,
shiny in the pines—I set this churl free,
like a pendragon
disappointed at the turnout,
and a little sad to see it go, but not
wanting to show this or to weigh it down
with my troubles, smiled
gaily for a couple
of the eighty or ninety minutes
it took the little ingrate to hightail it out of my yard.

About This Far

Still an unsolid customer,
piddler, careless among
sassafrass, lupine
and other ditch life on summer days
I set my bare feet among
to let the progesteronic heat
swallow my mind
as the sun itself etc in this preview
or what is it I am saying
will someday
those others to come in their turn
as when the speedy car
veers and goes
out of control, whipping us
into eternity where ox-eye daisies
and blue asters burn.

Meaty Chunks

If I ask forgiveness will the sweetgum tree
bend down to me, or cherries fall in my lap,
or the substitute driver,
the one who never liked us, will he honk compunctiously—
a man troubled in sleep by furious agents
of change—become like us
in a knowledgeable way? Will I become the one
who on the group campout makes potato pancakes
and later walks by the lake fretting about Mother,
dying of a tumor in Portland? *Where to?* ask
the oversubscribed,
turning for direction to self-published maps
scribbled over with rage.
The pride I thought so much of
has, if not abated, turned into a sleeping pill.
I gain through decrease,
like a goalie. And sit in my car eating raspberry glacé,
waiting for the singalong to begin. The top of something
wants to come off, but still
I back away, like a trainee before a bear with its head
in a bucket. Ludicrous, I think, sweating
and scared, ordered to continue with whatever it was I just forgot.

Leaves in the Subway

Breeze stirred by a train's
arrival lifts a green, yellow and pale red maple leaf,
spins and tosses it onto a bench where a woman in
dark blue like an old-fashioned governess moves down a bit to give it room.

The subtlety of forgiveness is more important and the twice-told
matter of a young girl's triumph in her software class,
stays with us longer, I suppose, and then we have the carefully
placed moments in which one who has made trouble all along,
in an unfashionable flourish
and a prank conceived out of a need to quell loneliness,
attempts to catch the attention of those in the know, and fails.

I've given religion much thought and now sometimes attend services.
I don't suppose it'll hurt, unless I meet
a malefic individual who gains influence and makes me
do illegal things. But this probably won't happen. I got caught
a few years ago in an internet scam, and
spent several months
retrieving my identity, but for a while now
I've been untouched by crime. The days mount like saucers on a table.
I give to charity when I think of it and try not to dwell
on where the money really goes; being kind is the idea, after all.

Yesterday I drove to the mall and walked around.
The young pear trees were just transferring their business to fall.
They looked nifty and neat, not too tall and free of messy fruit.
I thought of Stendhal in his late years, still working,
without much success, and of Follain and his penetrating
sight, young girls climbing French hills
to their big or little deaths, never having
indicated much or spoken. My wife and I are planning
a move to France. It'll be fun. Next week we'll visit the embassy
to chat about expectations and services. Out my window fall's
piecing things together, sweeping up
and generally preparing the park for winter. Soon we'll be sledding
on the white Paris hills. I have a new snowsuit and boots
and can't wait to try them out. It's another way of making friends.

Extremadura

I'm tired, spent really,
but don't say much, lean toward the rookeries, spirulina
days, effect trooperish refrains, undeliquent and pressed,
not hardy but persistent still, in a fading way,
feel dunked-on, put upon, dry-hearted often
in face of grief, bear trouble poorly, issue bulletins
to the Dept of the Interior
requesting stays and clarifications, sent to former
addresses. Querulous, taking too long to pee,
drafty, windy I mean, poised, or stuck, interested
in repellants,
chromium cures, provisional governments that stay on
forgetfully, crudely demanding
and ineffectual in a familiar way. Partial caps, vein splices,
unilateralisms, useful tips. Enormity
breaks through. The striation, evisceration of sunrise, dampened yellows
and parlous, disintegrating reds,
speedy particles stream, gravity, unspent grief, quivers at the fascia,
life a nolo contendere thing,
distent, then deflated, gurgling; raw winter fields,
boys kicking a football, a grainy, bottom-heavy mist almost too much
to bear, numb arguments pressed locally and taken
for universal truths, the next geezer over complaining,
or was that me, pushing at the fence that sags with our weight, and holds.

Chalk Pictures

Better, in the moment of application
when the fireball of impropriety or
failed deliverance, the inexcusable
act or defiance, the probative issue
related to the low-lit devilment dished
up by the local chapter, the pump
action love and refusal to commit
to a variance in affection, all these
stipulations and communards in their
best clothes standing by fire trucks
whistling light airs, to get going, better
to push right through the elemental
aspects, the universal complications
and hazardous cargo, apply a little
backyard chiffonade, minus lies,
forgo the shifts and decelerations,
and as the sun turns the moon to blue
sky, and birds sing, admit everything.

Pied Noir

At four I was put into steel-ribbed jackboots
in an attempt to shore up my ankles that they
said were too weak to hold me up on their own,
implausible, incomplete, half-wit mélanges,
frappés of bone and sinew, strapped into the
heavy oil-reeking burrow-like ordinance of my
black storm trooper boots that took twenty
minutes and all my tottish gifts to lace
up. I already knew how to read, having taught
myself by religiously studying the *Pogo* comic
books (Walt Kelly, artist) and so I knew from
the instructions, purpose and disclaimers
that accompanied the boots that these infernal
contraptions were designed to put the afflicted
child on equal footing with his peers. Equal
footing! Only if other children's feet were
set in cement. At once I knew that these clod
stompers were only another contrivance
conjured by my father to facilitate his task
of getting rid of me. Maybe he thought wearing
them would drive me to suicide—a laughingstock,
a humiliated person—or cause me to stumble
into traffic or provoke bullies to the point
that they would beat my head in with my

own steel-capped shoes. Nearly weeping,
grimacing with shame and unable entirely to
suppress his derisive laughter, Pop watched
with pornographic glee in his eyes as I laced
the leather pachyderms up. My choked-down
tears stung in my throat like Red Devil hot
sauce. In the backyard my mother shrieked
negatively, spewing her addled jazz. The
truth was I believed them. I accepted that
I was deformed, a local mutant who couldn't
walk straight or well. As I had raced barefoot
across lawns or dangled my feet in the
runoff creek I felt no pain or awkwardness.
But something must be wrong; they said so—
something invisible, something powerful
like the work of God, and it had warped
my toes and bent my ankles and stripped my
metatarsals of their power. At the same
time something else, a trashy, renegade
voice, only a tendency, a leniency, a notion,
rose in me. It rejected all the above
and suggested I was in the hands of killers.

Mistress of the Seas

You get started on say
a small business loan or love
affair and at first it
looks good the product's
imperishable or the lover
compels
with a startling emotional
accuracy you've not
known and so on
but still
you drop china or belligerently
oppose some
frightening contrivance a mislaid
sensibility like the wood duck's
symbolic
descent into the drained
marshland now a staging area for National
Guard maneuvers
and abruptly affection's
slathered with distaste the celebrated
sense of getting somewhere
begins to subside
like a tramp
steamer until at last you're back

on shore drenched sputtering
or dismally watching the *Mistress*
of the Seas and
so forth blubbering up
bubbles
and gulping as she sinks.

Angelus

The way the wind crosses the monument to Irish hunger
and enters Bronson Alcott's failed novel, pausing
to confirm the worst, loveless passages,
and carries on, humming behind the walls
of a lie first spoken by a tormented
usufructionist marooned in a crazy marriage outside Kiev,
and, after denting a thought just put into words
by Samuel Johnson, slips like an almost human hand
down the back of a roe deer, nearly
taming it for a sec, and splits into two parts along the Headland
of Shrouds in the Saint Lawrence Seaway, faltering,
descending, ruttling in the grass Popeye's
running through, simpering as it crosses
the desiccated hills of Jean Paul Belmondo's hometown,
raising a mutinous thought in one predisposed to depression,
edging palm groves in Kuala Lumpur and Fez,
diving for cover outside Camp Chiki-Wiki, the way the wind
places a foot on Buddhist graves in the Cimetière St-Vincent
and drags itself through Colette's dismal muttering,
tweaking the toes of her sandal-shod, hammer-toed feet,
saying nothing, promising nothing, refusing to fix
what's broken, leaving the hopeless to it and the jammed
and superseded falangists and masters

of evasive provisos, bringing nothing—fly-specked evacuated alcazar of zip—
to the beat-to-shit fathers who go on loving their no 'count sons,
and mothers the same, and to the sons,
dusting off their blown-away and run-down ridiculous hats.

Jargon

I got up early, winked at the wife,
went out and chopped a load of wood. I set the smoker
on its pins and got to work. This was

before I left for the airport. I thought
how bottomless that puddle looked
and shivered. You know how it is,

early, about 5 a.m., in downtown Havana,
before even the bums are awake? Well
it wasn't like that. I got some friendly advice

off the radio
and went back in to dress. The day looked like
something being inflated.

I found a picture in my mind
of boys rushing across the street to catch a glimpse
of a celebrity. Some-

one it would be in my best interest to know.
But then I remembered the smoker
and got the meat out of the fridge. "Honey," I called

to the old gal, who wouldn't be up for hours,
"remember to take the brisket off,"
and then I finished up and walked to the bus stop.

It is out of a morning such as this, filled with
intricate purple brushings
in the East, that Judgment Day will come.

The Greeks

I've been depressed lately about my general lack of advancement,
maybe that's it, nothing's coming out right,
and I thought man this is like a Greek tragedy,
but I read a book that said such business wasn't even ironic
and in most cases expected. I dream sometimes of going away,
but not as often as I used to, I've already cut out
so many times, started over, I don't know where I'd go
or don't trust—something, I stay where I am.
At the coffee bar where I go at daylight to work things through
a woman in straight-laced clothes comes in and goes out
nervously, asks for coffee, picks at her cuticles as she waits
looking around—I notice this
but it's as far as I go, the rounded cheeks, flat black eyes,
yes they're in there too, but no further than this, I don't speculate
for example about what's she's doing. I'm growing more numb as time
passes except for the moment when the person next to me is spoken to
and I become acutely embarrassed, like an adolescent who's sure
everyone can see through to his mucky shame. I see many others
who're weary and nervous and sore of heart,
but you can't speak to them in a city like this
without taking a chance on getting battered. Best to save
your tender feelings for the totally bamboozled, the foot-dragging
crumpled homeless guy who pulls himself hand over hand through the subway car
bleating and holding out his wrinkled paper cup. He's like us, metaphorically,

a man with work to do, getting on with it, some slaphappy liberator
God's taken up on the mountain and beat the shit out of
and sent back down sans a tablet of laws or any instructions whatsoever.
Now he's here, dopey and persistent, we know the story, we're part of it,
a bunch of Greeks the gods have turned their faces from,
we're down here on the grimy beach arguing and ruining everything,
getting up each day like men getting out of garbage bags behind the 7-Eleven,
hoping some beauty's beckoning, some version, unstable but plucky,
something safe and new, might show up. By now I've encountered
a thousand ways of looking at life, read books about it,
yet still I like to venture out at dawn
which even as it begins is ending, gray streets slumped
in fog. Sometimes I catch sight of a fresh compilation.
It's a variable, meaning. Then I notice in her old driver's license photo
the sadness in my ex-wife's face; it was there all the time.
She's out of the picture now, you might say,
off plumbing the atribilious instant out in LA. I remember waking up
after midnight thinking she's such a Nazi about the damn covers.
Wanting out, going into the bathroom to argue with myself,
nearly stupefied with regret that I'd ever married her.
Yet when it ended I cried for months. Is this Greek?
I don't know, human maybe. Everything's more tangled than ever.
Just now I'm thinking of old drunks, how their faces look doubled in size,
or the head shrunk, the skull back of the eyes,

brows tufty and separated by deep lines,

mouth slightly agape, lips slathered with a

purpose that's nearly faded out, the space between them shadowy

as if they've taken a small bite out of the dark

and hold it in their mouths, waiting for a drink to wash it down.

I'm minutes away from something important,

yet I don't know if I'll recognize it when it gets here.

Philoctetes, somebody, I think of him,

the wound that never heals, *there's* a story I could go for,

the slow stump up the beach toward the truth, or

maybe only the facts, some horrible revelation only minutes away.

Maybe stop for a donut or something, Phil, notice the pattern

if you can call it that, the windy momentum in the trees.

After Soon to Be

In dogged winter rain flat sheets of the *Courier &*
Intelligencer amid slurry of disintegration plus frail old
men out on Sunday and the brokenhearted and never-to-
resurface half-drugged and generally put upon ex-generalissimos
attempting to buck up ex officio lives yet the freshly
superior and duplicitous have to get up too poke
around open old suitcases looking for their "papers"
others thumbing through fortunes and digital
photos of Mississippi sunsets bottom-heavy houses
on grassy bluffs confused about where the ruction
took place down on one knee calling to the future praise
and dereliction—binding polymers—confusion racked
with secured manifestos disseminated by truck
and wireless device in vaporous morning
pale like an unstirred congee in which winter soon to
ratchet up the vig lies on its back in low spots
like a half wild dog amid sketchy buzz
of mental activity—call it that—sleeping undisturbed.

The Fall Schedule

The magisterial aspects of what's
left over are actually not enough
to foster the big-time proposals
you're looking for. A tent, white, filled
with musicians: that's what they
had in mind after the power failure. Love's,
that is. Foursquare and some episodes of
internal bleeding ago, we were almost
on top of things. The trees saw all
this in the way trees do, without saying
much. You got a light? I sat down
in the foyer like a protester, love's
strikeout artist, and decided to
devote myself to complicated matters.
The heat you feel's just the bodies
rotting underground. I thought that
up in the subway where once again
Car Seven was without a comeback.
You saw her calling for takeout,
but you didn't catch her name. I
mentioned this to the investigating
officers, but they were too exhausted
to pay attention. We'll get him
this time, they said, waving me away.

I thought I'd better go to Italy
or some place with old mismanaged fields
and sacks of potatoes stacked in
a barn by the woods where foxes
come out at night to romp in the grass.

The Adepts

The new day tunnels away under the oaks
and we see this,
see the shabby character and his religious radio,
the orthodox set of clouds above the park.
A few hang around speculating, getting over the night.
The rest are down on their knees praying
for forgiveness or for the triumph of their plans.
We're in tight with the dawn,
completely blown inside out, prostrate on the grass;
our shirts are burnt offerings,
our pants are carpets the priests walk on,
our bodies the sacrifice.

—*Please accept my night in jail, my hangdog expression,*
        the time I slept with my brother's wife;
please accept my desperate connivance, my
        loss of respect, the way I carried
three oranges in a sack until they rotted—

All around us the monks
and priests, the nuns of fun
go on with morning prayers.
A sister with a speckled face
scoops holy water from the fountain
and sprinkles it over our bent backs,

caws like a crow and offers
her body to the assistant
priest who is busy counting the take.

—Please accept my unhappy belly,
        my yellow toes; please accept
my cynical eyeballs and my variations on the theme
        of destitution; please accept
the nothing I am and the nothing I shall become—

There's a bustle in the oaks,
a stir in the maple trees;
the wind picks up. Jesus,
in the shape of a juicer,
gets out of the busted limo on the corner.
He hands out donuts,
steps into the bushes to pee.
God is the dog smell in his clothes,
the furtive look,
the broken fingers on his right hand,
the dirt filling in the lines on his palm.
God is the remains of memory
and the disconsolate muttering,
the braggadocio on the corner
who's as untrustworthy as he looks.

—it's a sunlit fruit peel, constant
reminders from the police,
the favoritism of certain officials,
dampened bread, the wet construction site
of her mouth, it's the fat
transvestite at the spigot
undressing down to her manhood
shaved pink as a baby's,
and the one-legged pigeon Mother Superior
chases with a broken umbrella.

—*Please accept my lack of belief,*
   my war with decomposition;
please accept my utter disregard
   for the ornamental
arrangements, the displaced,
   overlooked and sometimes eerily
unavailable
   creed we all live by,
the scrap upon which is written
   the one true word—

Whatever you have,
says the peculiar and dusty God,
I want that.

Kingdom

I lay my hand on your chest
and for a sec can't feel anything

       tin roof
       on an empty cotton shed

late winter
       in the ruined kingdom
              of the fields
no approach saintly

the register tallying a number
unfathomable to scientists
             or lovers

       turns taken
       brisk wind at the corner of Washington
       and Spanish Way

old men pretending
the dark's holding steady

another marooned in a philosophy

junk

or tricky love affair

we say tenderness
still seek restitution
                    anything you can name
                                        or not

the numbers add up
they say

and Forestall, Kissinger, Old Brezhnev
friends with cold fingertips
you say

        consider the fractions

necessary components

and something like a basket of leaves
fresh, green

        the able-bodied have moved away

I lay my hand on your chest

     a stillness in the woods
     in the fields

Unburnt Offerings

Day knocks back in yellows and bright
levantine blues, thin shades of a color lost to the Mayans,
rediscovered over St Pete around six. Vacations

rescinded, interrupted by a solemn episode, a few words at a grave.
Carefully, with no intent
to harm, two brothers break into the back of Saul's Electrical Supply,

looking for gimmicks. Friends of a lifetime wake
separately in unfamiliar beds, choking on guilt. *Reconciliation*
comes too soon, a woman thinks and turns back to her dream.

A famous toastmaster, eating from a sack of *churros*,
decides to leave his wife for the love of a good man. The mayor
checks his bulldog's teeth. *Pain's my name*,

the ER doctor says, *or, no—my game*, he says—*oh gosh*,
and falls off the toilet with a heart attack. *Infarction*, his six-year-old whispers
as he takes out the garbage, and looks up at the sky where something

heretofore impossible to get a handle on seems to be separating itself from the casual
run of clouds.
Grapefruit pulp coats the back wheels of a delivery truck on Stock Street.

A young man attempting to memorize
a paragraph from the *Call & Appeal* recalls what
he meant to say at the confab, a quote from

Francis Bacon concerning the indefatigabilty of—*what was it?* A policeman,
fossicking his wife's vagina, decides to come clean. *Sweetness,*
the child model thinks, that's what keeps me going. Or do I mean *tendresse?*

Clean

Flattened, sprawled out, snuffling like a dog,
I sniff the expectorate and the feculent lost phenomena,
the shavings and culls, the drifted apart discards
and answers become complications heaved into the grass.
I slide on my belly over the damp places
where old men lay down to try the earth on for size.
In misused areaways behind buildings, among the grassy footings
and slippery spots where disgusting practices ended up, I find
a kind of happiness. My body's covered with what's down there.
Mottled and stained, I've become one with the particulate, the crumb,
the soiled and ineradicable section, the sulcated and unattended spot.
I follow the hog trail of longing. The lowdown is my fortune.
The fundament, the footing, the radicle, the rhizoid, the parquet.
Mouth stuffed with dirt, I chew the bulletins of governance and desire
and take comfort in the filth, in the place
of failure and exudation. I am at home among fistulas
and burned patches, down there with the stems, the shrieks that failed
to arouse pity, the exogenous hopes tossed out with the trash.
What I gather about me was there before I came.
It is often slick and pulpy like a mango,
hot like the scrap of cat hide the sun shines on,
and in its capacity to represent the likelihood of a life beyond
integrity and consummation, I am solaced.
I make small flapping motions, I scurry

my feet and spirate, dragging myself forward,

paying a manifest attention to the tiny voices of ant wings and drying spittle,

and I repeat what they say. In the faint resettlings

of dust and endlessly reducible fractions

I recognize my own voice. Like them I am not saying anything important.

Like them—like the torn-off bee abdomens and locust petals,

the crusts—I have left behind the designs

and purposes I was built for. I am free to inch along,

without meaning. Among the lost

I'm found. I present to myself the unoccupied remainders and

disarranged failed circumstances, the painted tin receptacles

and scuffed flooring of transience: among the discarded, discarded:

among the deserted, the marooned, the forsook, I am part of things.

Now the casual elimination is acceptable to me,

the object hurled down in fury or bitterly tossed aside,

the letter torn to pieces,

the wedding ring in feckless ceremony placed

between two slightly larger stones and covered with moss,

the torn away excess

and deliveries that failed to reach their destinations—

all are acceptable, as are the messy discharges and the exuviation.

Relinquishments, the scattering of pieces, erasures and jettisons,

the fatally incomplete, are equal in my sight.

I flutter and scramble, I drag myself overhand,

leaving a trail, abreast of the trash,

keeping up with dereliction, equal with the failed repairs,

the designs growing more marginal as we speak.

It is here I find the endings that in their perfections of absolute loss

have become beginnings again, the bitten-off phrases and

inconspicuous wadding of spoiled opportunity about to start over.

I see the lost revamped. The mortified recast.

The crapped out recombined with the useless to make the futile.

All the old possibilities—corrigendious, bone-headed and radiant—are here.

Compensation

. . . tiptap slips, hammer blows, all obvious, no nonsense,

make-right work, boys go crazy . . . *You press her hard,* she says,

you can see her mind overheat, the madness flood her . . .

dreams of summer in midwinter Manhattan, trash spills

out bins, white streaks, boys sleep on salt piles,

no resistance after a while, we give in,

to loneliness, to pain, to the devil and indulgence,

all life a contortion pressed through a slot

in time, remnants fall, crumbs that become

ponds in city parks, trees stained gold by autumn sun, love's cha-cha-cha.

ACKNOWLEDGMENTS

Some of these poems appeared in the following journals: *Bloomsbury Review, Five Points, Grand Street, Hunger Mountain, The Kenyon Review, Luna, NYCBig CityLit.com, Open City, The Nation, The New Republic, The Paris Review, Pleiades, Ploughshares, Poetry, The Southern Review, Tin House, TriQuarterly, Volt, Western Humanities Review.* Thanks to the editors and staff.

Many thanks to the MacDowell Colony for fellowships during which several of these poems were written.